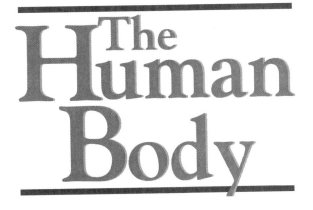

The Human Body

Photo Credits:

The Human Body

by
Stacy Savran

Scientific Consultant
Paul H. Penzer, M.D.

kidsbooks®
INCORPORATED

Making a Human Body

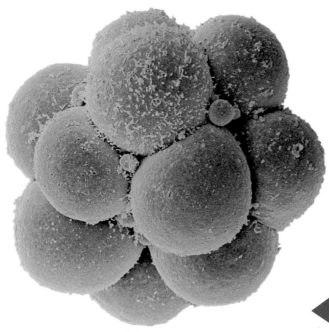

Do you know how you came to be? A tiny *cell* from your father joined a cell inside your mother. This unit started dividing into many cells. Cells are like building blocks—they build a human body.

◀ *These cells are dividing to make a human being.*

A baby growing inside its mother is called a fetus *(FEE-tus)*. As the baby gets bigger, so does the mother's belly!

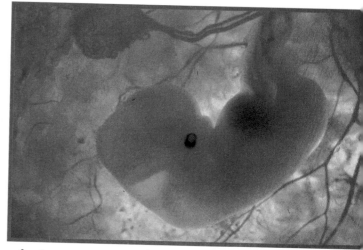

A two-month-old fetus

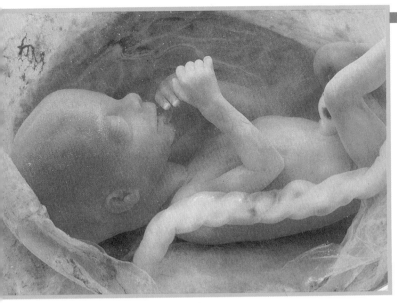

A fetus is connected to its mother by a tube. Food and oxygen (OX-ih-jen), pass through the tube to help the fetus grow.

A four-month-old fetus

 **Q&A** **Which parts of my body grow the fastest?**

Your finger-nails, toenails, and hair grow the fastest. In fact, they never stop growing!

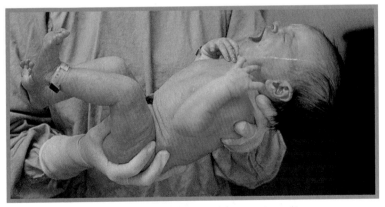

After about nine months, the baby is born.

Watch Me Grow!
Place your hand on a piece of paper and draw around it. Write the date on it. Every month, draw your hand again. Compare the pictures. Are you getting bigger?

Outside and Inside

You are special because there is no one else like you in the whole world. You look different from any other person— unless you're an *identical twin.* Identical twins are two people who are born at the same time and look exactly alike.

Even if you do not have a twin, you have many things in common with other humans. On the outside, you have hair and skin, hands and feet, a head with two eyes, two ears, a mouth, and a nose. On the inside, you are built of many amazing things—bones, muscles, and *organs* like the brain and heart.

What's the largest organ in my body?

Believe it or not, it's your skin!

ON THE OUTSIDE

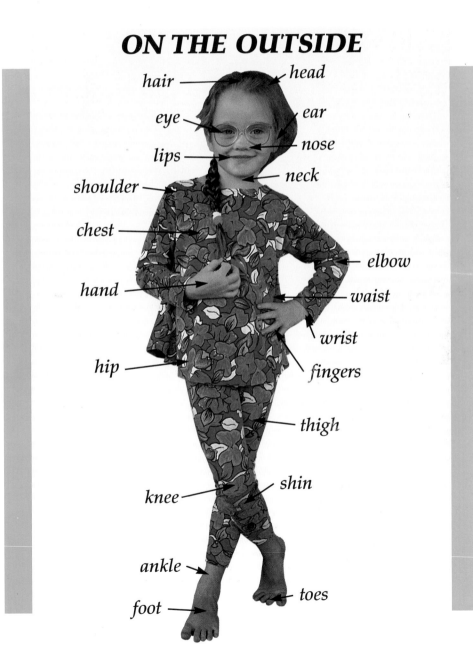

hair — head

eye — ear

nose

lips — neck

shoulder —

chest —

elbow

hand — waist

wrist

hip — fingers

thigh

knee — shin

ankle —

foot — toes

Stretchy Skin

Your body is covered with soft, stretchy skin that grows as you grow. It protects the inside of your body by keeping out water, sunlight, and germs.

It also keeps you warm or cools you down.

Melanin (MEH-lah-nin) gives your skin its color—lighter skin has less melanin, and darker skin has more. Melanin protects your skin from harmful sun rays. In some people, it also makes freckles!

Q&A **How does a cut heal?**
First, blood dries over the cut making a scab. The scab keeps germs out while new skin cells grow. Then the scab falls off. A bandage helps a scab protect a cut.

Skin Clue!
No one has the same *fingerprint* as you. Press your thumb on an ink pad. Then press your thumb on a piece of paper. That's your fingerprint!

Bony Body

What gives your body its shape? Your bones, all 206 of them! Together, these bones make up a hard *skeleton* that protects you and helps you move.

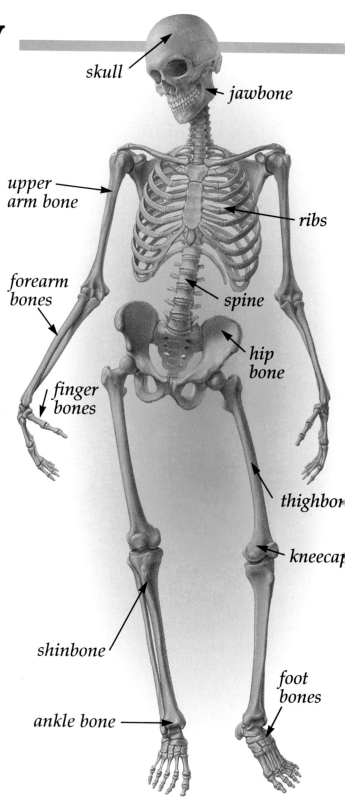

skull

jawbone

upper arm bone

ribs

forearm bones

spine

finger bones

hip bone

thighbo[r]

kneecap

shinbone

ankle bone

foot bones

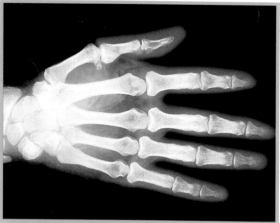

A photograph of your bones is called an X ray.

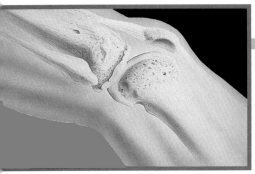

A knee joint

Your bones connect at *joints.* Joints are places that bend, such as your knuckles, elbows, and knees.

Open and close your mouth. You just used your *jawbone.* Teeth grow from your jawbone. Babies grow 20 *milk teeth.* These "baby" teeth fall out when you're about seven, and 32 *adult teeth* take their place.

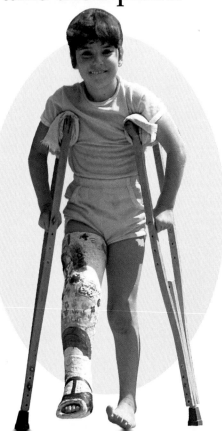

 **What happens if a bone breaks?**

A broken bone can mend itself. A cast protects the bone as it heals.

Make a Muscle

Muscles work with your bones to get your body moving. Food, fresh air, and exercise help muscles grow and get stronger.

There are about 650 muscles in your body. Each has a different job to do. The muscles in your toes help you walk. The muscles in your face help you smile!

Some of your muscles move when you want to use them—like the ones in your arms. Other muscles, like your heart and stomach, move on their own to get their jobs done.

You move muscles even when you smile!

Flex!

To "make a muscle," bend your arm at the elbow. This is called *flexing*. The flexed muscle between your elbow and shoulder is called your *biceps* (BI-seps). It is used for lifting and pulling.

Q&A **Which muscle do I use to talk?**
You use your tongue—it's not just for tasting! It's a strong muscle that moves to form different words and sounds.

Big Brain

Inside your head, you have a brain. Right now, it's about the size of your two fists. But your brain grows as you get bigger.

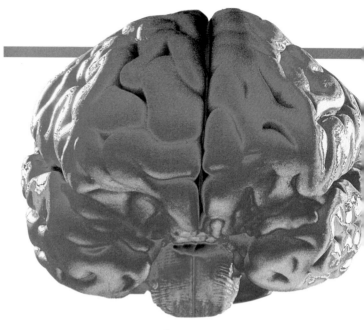

▲ *A human brain*

You *think* with your brain. You think when you use your imagination or do homework.

A,B,C... What comes next? Ask your brain! It *memorizes*, or learns, things like the alphabet.

Did you know that your brain is in charge of your whole body? Messages travel to and from the brain on pathways called *nerves*.

When you play outside, messages from the brain tell your legs to run or to jump.

All your nerves are connected to your brain.

Q&A **Why do I dream?**
Some people think we dream so our brain can catch up on what we did during the day.

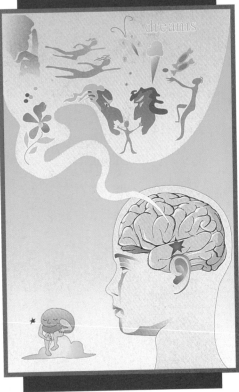

Use Your Brain!
Look at these numbers and then close the book. See if you can remember the order of the numbers when you are not looking at them:

1 2 3 4 5 4 3 2 1

Seeing and Hearing

Your senses tell you about the world around you.

Seeing

Eyes are for seeing colors and images.

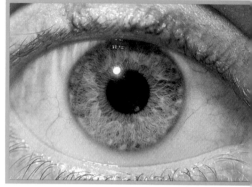

The colored part of th eye is called the iris.

Light enters your eye through the *cornea*—a kind of protective window. Light then goes through the *pupil,* a small black hole.

A *lens* focuses light on the *retina*. From there messages travel to the brain. The brain makes pictures so you know what you're seeing!

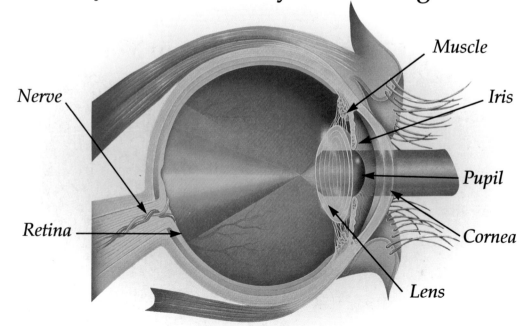

Muscle

Nerve

Iris

Pupil

Retina

Cornea

Lens

Q&A **Why do some people need eyeglasses?**
Sometimes the lens inside the eye does not work well. Eyeglasses help out and make things clearer.

Hearing

Music and other sounds travel in waves. Soundwaves enter a small tunnel in your ear called the *ear canal.* The waves pass from your *eardrum* to tiny bones in the *middle ear.* Then, in your *inner ear,* nerves pick up the soundwaves and send messages to your brain. Your brain tells you what you are hearing.

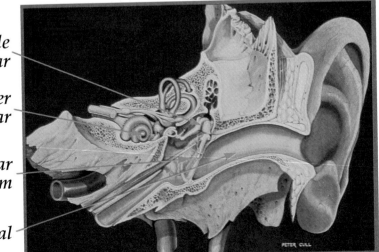

Middle Ear

Inner Ear

Ear Drum

Ear Canal

Smelling and Tasting

When you eat an ice-cream cone, your nose smells it and your tongue tastes it.

Your tongue tastes food that is sweet, sour, salty, or bitter. It has tiny bumps on it called *taste buds.* They send messages to the brain.

Smells enter your nose through your nostrils. ny hairs inside ur nose pass e smells to a erve. The nerve rries the smells your brain, hich may say, Hey, it's a ower!"

Touching

What happens when a butterfly lands on your arm? You can feel it because of the nerves under your skin. You can feel that something is hot or cold, soft or hard, rough or smooth. You can also feel pain, like when you stub your toe.

Test Your Touch

Ever play Blindman's Bluff? It's a game in which a blindfolded player tries to catch another player. The Blindman then tries to identify the player by touching his or her face.

Heart and Blood

Your heart is a strong muscle in your chest. It's about the size of your fist. It pumps blood and never gets tired. Your heart pumps, or *beats*, about 70 times a minute. When you run, it beats faster.

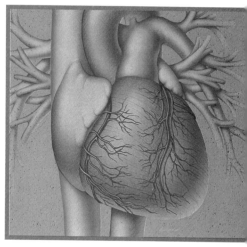

When blood leaves your heart, it goes through tubes called *arteries*. Arteries carry the blood to all parts of your body. *Veins* carry blood back to your heart.

◄*Arteries are shown in red, and veins in blue.*

Q&A

What is blood?

Blood is mostly water and *red cells*. Water helps blood move. Red cells carry oxygen. Blood also has *white cells*, which fight germs, and *platelets*, which heal cuts.

In this picture, red cells are red, white cells are yellow, and platelets are pink.

Feel the Beat!

Put your hand in the middle of your chest and feel your heart. Now jump up and down. Feel your heart again. Is it beating faster?

Breathing

You breathe air in and out all the time without even thinking about it! Air has oxygen which your body needs to live.

 **Q&A** **What are hiccups?**

Sometimes air rushes into your lungs. A flap in your throat snaps shut—Hic! And then opens again—Cup! There are tricks to stop hiccups, but usually they go away naturally.

With air from your lungs, you can blow bubbles and whistles.

You breathe in through your nose and mouth. Air goes down your wind-pipe and into your lungs. Blood in your lungs picks up

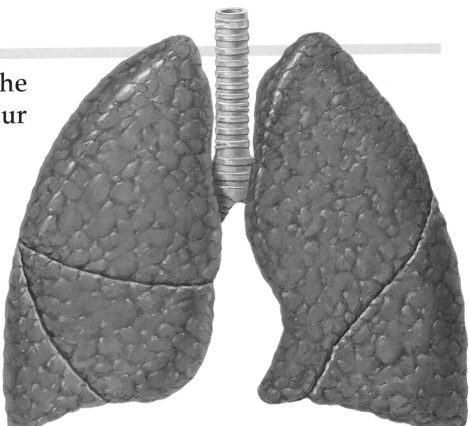

the oxygen and carries it to the rest of your body.

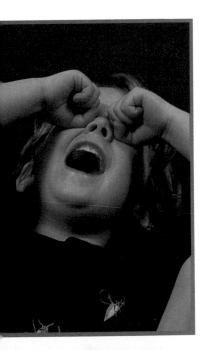

Sometimes your body tries to get more air to keep you awake. That's when you yawn!

Air moving out of your body over your voice box helps you talk or whistle.

All Puffed Up!

Get an idea of how your lungs fill up with air and empty out. First, blow up a balloon. Then let the air out slowly.

Digestion

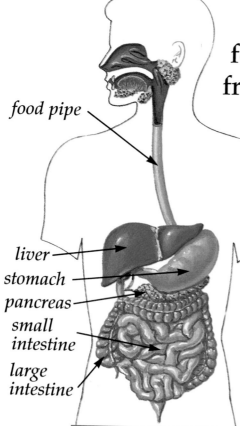

food pipe

liver
stomach
pancreas
small
intestine
large
intestine

Digestion is a fancy word for how your body gets energy from food. It starts with chewing. Your teeth and saliva, or spit, break up food into small pieces. Next, you swallow. The food goes down your food pipe into your stomach. The stomach squeezes to mix the food with special juices.

Next, the mushy food moves through your intestines. There, vitamins are taken from the food into your blood.

Any food or water not used by your body is called waste. Waste leaves you when you go to the bathroom.

Water is important to your body.

Q&A **Why does my stomach growl?**

All your stomach juices are rumbling around, digesting. Your stomach rumbles even louder when it is empty and looking for food!

Food Fun!

There are four food groups. Can you guess which ones are found in a cheese pizza? Don't forget the tomato sauce!

1) fruit and vegetables

2) meat, fish, eggs (protein)

3) milk, cheese, butter (dairy)

4) bread, rice, potatoes, pasta (grains)

Answer: vegetables (tomato sauce), dairy (cheese), and grains (bread)

Keeping Healthy

How do you keep your body working right? Give it the things it needs!

Water helps things like blood move easily through your body.

Good food gives you energy.

Exercise makes your muscles strong.

Sleep is important to help you grow.

Brushing your teeth helps them stay clean and strong.

Bathing keeps germs away.

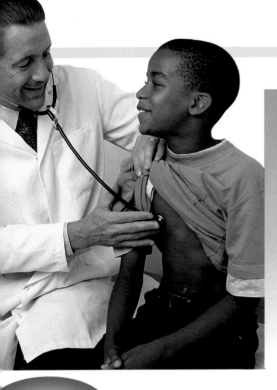

Visiting the Doctor

A doctor gives you a check-up to make sure everything is working right. With a *stethoscope*, the doctor listens to your heart and lungs.

Q&A **What causes chicken pox?**

Not chickens! It's a disease caused by a virus and lasts about a week. The itchy pox are small, red marks on your skin.

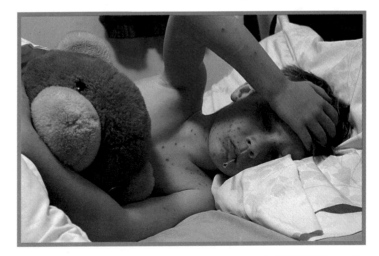

Hot or Cold!

Ask an adult to take your temperature with a *thermometer*. Your body temperature should be around 98.6 degrees. A higher temperature is a *fever*. A fever tells you that your body is sick and needs rest.